Dundalk Proud

Poems and Slices of Life by
W. H. Stevens
Lite Circle Books
Baltimore, Maryland
June 2004

Lite Circle Books
P.O. Box 26162
Baltimore, MD 21210
(410) 889-1574
website: www.litecircle.com
e-mail: lite@toadmail.com

Lite Circle Books is a division of *The Lite Circle, Inc.*, a non-profit literary association devoted to the encouragement of emerging voices in the arts. Please write for more information.

To Order Additional Copies of:
Dundalk Proud
Poems and Slices of Life by W. H. Stevens
Send check or money order (in US funds) made out to
<u>*Lite Circle, Inc.*</u> **for <u>$11</u> for <u>each book</u> ordered to:**

Lite Circle Books: *Dundalk Proud*,
P.O. Box 26162, Baltimore, MD 21210

Poems & Photographs, Copyright 2004 Wendy Hellier Stevens

Published 2004 by Lite Circle Books, P.O. Box 26162, Baltimore, MD, 21210, (410) 889-1574, www.litecircle.com

Typeset & Design by Win-Cri Enterprises

Library of Congress Cataloging-in-publishing Data:
Dundalk Proud/ W. H. Stevens

Library of Congress Control Number: 2004105051

ISBN 0-9641622-6-1

Printed in the United States of America

All rights reserved under International and Pan-American copyright conventions. No part of this book may be reproduced, stored in a retrieval system, or transmitted in any form, electronic, mechanical, or other means, now known or hereafter invented – except for brief quotes in reviews – without written permission from The Lite Circle, Inc. and/or the author.

In Memory of my Father,
William W. Hellier, Sr.

Acknowledgements

A sincere note of gratitude to the following wonderful people in my life who made this book a reality: To my husband and best buddy, Robert F. Stevens for his love and support; to my children Patrick T. Stevens and Mary A. Stevens for all of their love and understanding; to my dear friend and sister Vonnie Winslow Crist who has encouraged me since day one; to David Kriebel and Patti Kinlock who saw the value of my work; to my writer friends: Marta Knobloch, Stacy Tuthill, and Danuta Kosk-Kosika; and finally to Bob Gattuso, Jim Davis, and Ed Peppler who were professional guides and to Wilson Watson, who taught me the value of writing.

The following publications and their editors published many of my poems that are included in this book. Without their support I would never have had this collection. My thanks to them for giving me the opportunity to express myself and I urge everyone to support large and especially small presses. Thank you to: *The Baltimore Sun, The Baltimore Review, The Maryland Poetry Review, Lite: Baltimore's Literary Monthly, Wordhouse, Fodderwing, Robin's Nest, Spotlights The Harford Poet, The Liriodendron Review, Chesapeake, Late Knocking, The Pen Woman Magazine, The Plastic Tower, Parnasus Literary Journal, The Towson University Towerlight, Chimeras, Troubadour's Digest, Poetic Page, Lower Than the Angels, Through A Glass Darkly, Digges Choice, A Seal Upon My Heart, Pegasus Review, Function at the Junction #2,* and *Harford County Dimensions.*

Table of Contents

May 27th	3
Night Train	4
Tracks In the Snow	5
Dundalk Proud	6
Fourth of July	7
Mystery Beauty	8
Avon Lady	9
Cousin Maddie	10
Eastpoint Expedition	11-12
Sweet Taste of Summer	15
Watermelon Feast	16
Escape From the Point	17-18
Union Man	19
The Sunbathers	20
The Good Humor Man	21
Approach	22
The Shearing	23-24
Linguistics	25
Church Talk	26-27
On Creativity	28
Flying With Sandra	29
Opal Tears	30
Easter 1957	33-34
Alice	35
Grief Has A Sound	36
Vixen Hill	37
Vigil	38
Walking At Holly Hill	41
Painted Daisies	42
Prophets	43-44
If Only	45

Table of Contents

Words	46
Night Watchman	47-48
Louisville Slugger	49
Red Carpet Treatment	50
Mole Lady	53
Kentucky Derby Clock	54
Ivory Tower	55-56
Slick Raymond	57
Dundalk Sabbath	58
Dundalk Cowboys	59
Our Heroes	60-61
Luzon 1944	62
Paper Boat	65
Obits and Pieces	66-67
Down the Avenue	68
Matinee	69-70
Sideshow	71
Clover Chains	72
North Point A La Carte	75-76
Patapsco Portrait	77-78
Lessons	79
Fantasy	80
Balticon '96	81
Une Tranche de Vie	82
Bilingual	83
Boudicca	84
Winter Solstice	85
After the Storm	86
About *Dundalk Proud*	87-88

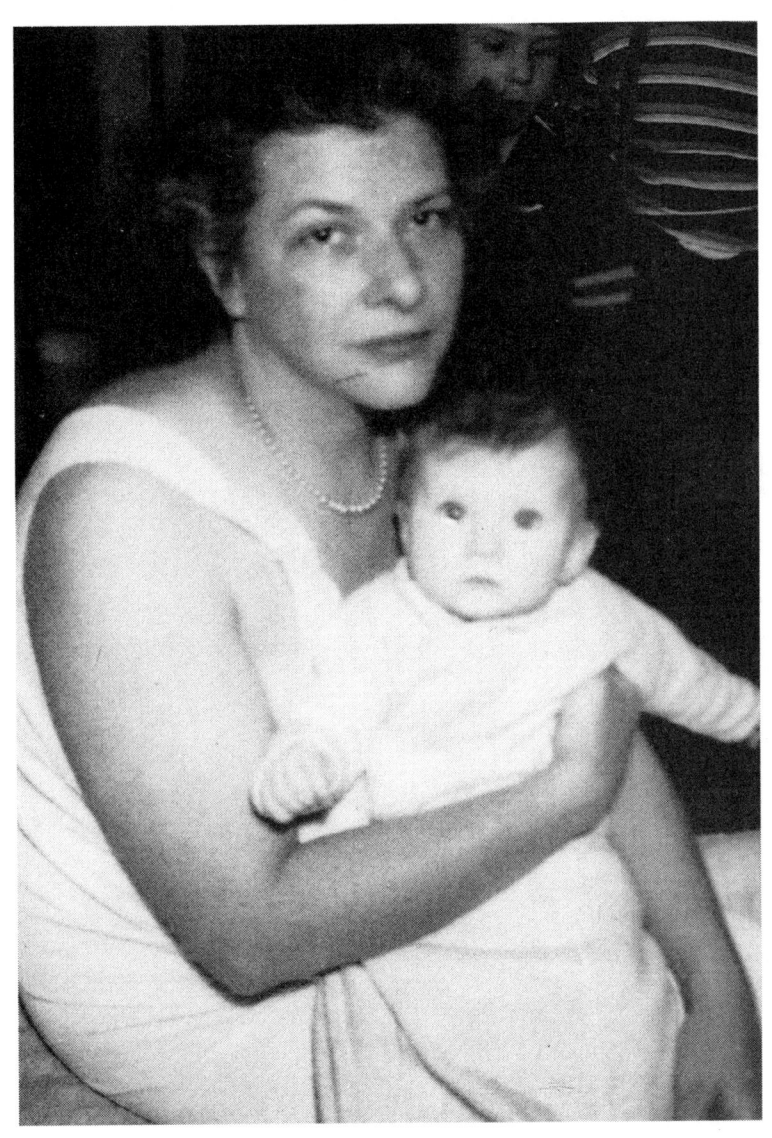

"Every blade of grass has its Angel that bends over it and whispers, "grow, grow."" -- The Talmud

May 27th

Angel fingers have woven
my life up a ladder
of birthdays. Annually,
acolytes with faces
starched like doilies
have lit candles
fire-polished to perfection.
Each facet is tucked
away in fine cool linen,
in preparation for
a Hope Chest.

Today, a soft watercolour
wash embraces me.
The sun bursts through
a cathedral of leaves
as a choir sings from
lofty nests.

It smells like rain
among the cedar trees.
The air is fresh and sweet.
I breathe, I breathe.

Night Train

Were you the
keeper of deep
family secrets
in those days
when you
swaddled your
children about
you -- lips
full as a
blooming iris,
lonely as a cloud?
Was I a happy
accident or the
foil of best laid
plans, conceived
in a night coach
en route to Baltimore?
A spreading scarlet
wound hidden in
folds of flannel,
I was always ready
to jump back into
the busy pink
wallpaper of
your bedroom.
Your pleading eyes
provoked my thoughts.
I wanted to ask
you last time we
talked, but my tongue
couldn't keep up
with my mind.

Tracks In the Snow

One day from the end
of her sleeve,
she realized that
her hand looked familiar,
the wrinkles across her knuckles
and the raised blue veins,
long expressive fingers
with not so perfect nails -
short and clean they were.
Loosely her wedding ring climbed
one finger reflecting
her mother's face
and then her own.
She turned her hand over.
The palm held etchings of life
that disappeared
like tracks in the snow.

Dundalk Proud

(dedicated to Kimbel E. Oelke)

Every Wednesday over on Dundalk Avenue
in the dingy smoke-filled Eagle newsroom,
manual Smith-Coronas spat out copy
up to deadline, telephones rang till
they fell off their greasy perches.
Our Heroes, The Mystery Beauty Contest,
and Dun-Talk, along with News Brevities
and classifieds, were blue-lined,
X-Acto knifed, then pigeon-holed
onto waiting flats, camera ready,
then put to bed.

Crammed with Our Churches,
weddings and obits, juxtaposed
with police reports, petty crimes,
and fender-benders,
it roosted in mailboxes and news stands
each Thursday, feathering the nests
of a community steeped in tradition and
pride like the Annual Heritage Day Parade
held on the Fourth of July.

Fourth of July

The air was
laced with steamed
crabs and beer
as we gathered webbed
chairs in somnolent
shadows of latticed
sunlight. The scent
of Citronella candles
loitered in the
summer dusk.
Above the high
tension wires,
a pageant wider than
angels' wings
exploded; a hornet's
nest flung across
the sky.
Our faces,
bathed in sequins,
we witnessed a
spectacle that
rivaled a welder's
torch. Each
spark flayed above
us, then cascaded
like hot tears
to the ground.
Soft as the whispers
of the extinguished
candles, the dusty
silence announced
its finale.

The Mystery Beauty Contest

Who is she? I know!
It's LaVerne DuPray –
the manicurist at Marge's Salon
on Holabird Avenue.
You know LaVerne – she's
got platinum-teased hair
and those new cat eye glasses
that are all the rage.
If we're lucky, we'll be
one of the first ten callers
and we can look just like her!
Remember last week the
Mystery Beauty was Virginia Snell –
You know – she's the secretary
at North Point Junior High.
Why they chose her, I'll never know.
But my friend, Joanne, won
a free shampoo and set last Friday…
Anyway, all I know is for a week
Virginia acted all snooty and
full of herself because she thought
she was Queen of Dundalk!
So at two on Friday
I'm gonna be on that phone
because LaVerne DuPray is the
Mystery Beauty.
This week I'll get through
and I'll be the one in the
stylist's chair getting the
works at Grove's.
Why, the Eagle might recognize
my potential and feature me
in their contest next week!

Avon Lady

We were told only
whores wore blue
eye shadow and black
mascara; a little
powder or rouge, but
none of that eye stuff!

Genteel Miss Martha's
gloved hand dipped into
her black satchel, full
of sample tubes of lipstick,
face creams and Chiclets
for us curious girls.

She smelled of roses,
or lilacs or maybe
lilies of the valley,
her proper-coiffed hair
hugged her porcelain cheeks.

Our eyes widened at the
variety of specials in
Miss Martha's dog-eared
brochure, we dreamt of
being beautiful.

Now, I stroke
on black mascara, the
forbidden fruit, close
my blue eyes, toss
back my head, I laugh just
like a wicked harlot.

Cousin Maddie

On Christmas Eve, my atheist cousin, Maddie,
mysterious sinister siren of the family,
fluid as ink, seeped into the living room,
poured herself into Uncle Rick's easy chair.

With a wicked Jane Seymour smile, she
fingered dozens of frayed dreadlocks with
jeweled black nails till they scaled about
her thin shoulders like Medusa.

Her bloodstone eyes, cold as agates,
peered over her sunglasses, and when
she laughed, her earrings cascaded along
her slender white neck, rattling like
skeletons on Hallow's Eve.

At the stroke of twelve, the night held
its breath when Maddie, dripping with
darkness, slipped back onto East Eden Street
where they say she conversed with serpents
about men's souls as she slithered in the
gutters under the wheels of parked cars.

Eastpoint Expedition

"We're goin' home,
an' that's that,"
Mom hissed. Grabbed
me by the arm, shoved
me on the escalator.
Big sister Sharon,
overwhelmed by shopping
bags, froze behind us
on the steely threshold.

Jagged metallic fangs
struck out at her toes.
The staircase slithered
downward, a silvery,
scaly, wicked predator.

The slick staircase slid
quickly, silently from
sight beneath the floor
below. It was too much.
Bags flew everywhere
followed by a piercing
acrophobic shriek.

I cried out, too,
for Sharon was about
to be eaten alive.
The hungry jaws
gnashed their teeth.

Then it all stopped.

Shoppers gaped, Mom
shrinking into her
shoes, lividly shoved
us into a North Point Cab
with no shocks,
dirty springless seat.

A worse beating waited
at home, for we had
caused her shame.

Sweet Taste of Summer

Hot July afternoons filled
      the Carnival glass pitcher.
Red soft drink mix and sugar
      stirred with a long wooden spoon.
Days went by as quickly as
      ice cubes melting into
that sweet taste of summer.

Watermelon Feast

One hot city day
when the A-rab
sold fresh produce
from his pony cart,
Mom bought a
big, ripe, watermelon.
After a morning
chilling it in the
Fridgidaire, she
sliced plate-sized
wedges for all
the neighbor-kids.
They gorged themselves
on the back cellar
wall, peppered
the pavement with
the seeds, watched
ants congregate
around each one
till the walk
looked like a
Dalmatian's coat.
Cold, sticky juice
ran down their
chins, elbows, legs.
Susan grabbed
the hose, turned
on the spigot.
Native sons danced
in the rainbow of
that cold, cold spray.

Escape From the Point

As kids, we went on a
Sunday School picnic
at Patapsco State Park.
Armed with baseball
bats and mitts, we
rode a beat-up yellow
bus that stalled on
hills, moaned when
the gears were shifted.
Out in the woods,
on big rocks, we dined
on peanut butter,
slapped our legs to
ward off the bugs,
tromped the trails
in Bermudas and Keds,
caught terrible cases
of poison ivy
climbing the trees.
The Swinging Bridge was
our biggest challenge.
A scary, awesome structure
suspended by frayed, hairy
ropes stretched over a ravine.
It swayed uneasily with
the slightest movement.
We could see the drop below
through the wooden slats.

With ginger steps, we inched.
It creaked under our weight,
trembled, quivered, whined.
Each dubious plank was tested.
We stared at the bottomless
abyss below, mouth open
waiting to devour us whole,
never to be seen again.
By day's end, we knew.
So we scampered across
the conquered bridge,
unwary, trusting, confident.
Itchy, sunburned city kids,
gathered dusty equipment,
bottles of Sea and Ski squashed
futilely flat into brown grocery bags.
The sweaty, jerky bus
coughed up the road
back into the "Point,"
A Hundred Bottles of Beer
on our lips.

Union Man

Kitty's dad worked
down the 'Point.
Came home yesterday
with big long burns
across the palms
of his calloused hands.

Seems with worn safety
gloves, Norm had inspected
one pipe too many in
the sweltering August mill.

The taste of red dust
in his mouth, he washed
it away with a swig of
National Boh, turned on
the ball game. Fell
asleep next to the radio,
satisfied with his lot.

Last fall, big on Union,
they all struck.
That rusty powder stuck
to their front porch,
stifling hopes, aspirations.

Kitty didn't get a doll
that Christmas for there
wasn't even enough money
to buy the foil icicles
for their tree.

The Sunbathers

"The summer is your enemy,"
Mom used to say, but we
never listened. Fair-skinned
and freckled, we laid on
the porch, white linen drying
in the sun -- it was so warm,
the air so crisp, but at day's
end, Mom, smirking under her
wide-brimmed hat was right.
The red sun set, but we
remained steaming; eggs
over easy on the walk.

Good Humor Man

The Good Humor man
jangled his bells.
Parents treated him
like a neighborhood
pestilence, but to the
kids, he was the
Pied Piper.
One evening, little
Trixie heard the
bells as she took
her bath, jumped
from the tub,
ran down the street
yelling, "Wait a
minute!" for she
wanted to be first
in line. He'd run
out of cherry Popsicles
last time. Got clear
out to the curb, didn't
have her five cents
or her clothes.

Approach

They say if you
peel an onion
far enough...
Concentric circles
are the same.
The inner most circles
are the most intimate.
I'm not an onion
nor the center
of a circle.
It's time, not space
that makes the
difference.
Only a slight sound
and birds will fly,
a rabbit will dart
into the forest.

The Shearing

When Marcy was six,
blonde waves flowed
to her waist.

Each day, Miss Rue
curled Marcy's locks
with her fingertip.
Ran a fine-toothed
comb through the
thick tangles.

Marcy'd cry, Miss
Rue'd slap 'er,
tell 'er to shut up,
raked the comb harder.

Marcy yelled one
time too many that
mornin', so Miss
Rue, she grabbed
some dull iron clippers,
lopped off handfuls
of silky curls.
Flung 'em in an old
brown paper Acme bag.
For good measure, Rue
smacked Marcy upside
the head with the heavy
black handles of
those wretched shears.
Sent 'er to school
lookin' like a scarecrow.

"Served 'er right," laughs
Rue to this day, remembering
the date, the color of the comb
and the name of the store
emblazoned across the
bag in big red script.

Over forty-five years
later, Marcy brushes
her long, golden hair.

She remembers, too.

Linguistics

It's like placing direct object pronouns
in correct order as I study a foreign language.
I struggle with each new word when you call.
When I hear it's you, I dig my fingernails
into my palms, my stomach reminds me of
the guilt that ate my happiness; how you
ladled it on with big helpings of lies.

Long ago, I broke my silence. You were
light with my words. They floated from
your mouth till everyone had caught them
one by one on their tongue-tips, like
snowflakes in winter. Confused and sad,
I couldn't sort them out -- the subjects and
verbs didn't agree, the syntax was all wrong.

Your quicksilver tongue is honey
poured on pain. No longer fluent,
I push my words way back in my head,
till they reach the vanishing point.

Church Talk

Look. There's Marcy's family.
Over there, right in front,
is Linda with her grandson,
Donnie, on her lap.
They don't know who his
daddy is – his mother
is a prostitute doing time
in the county detention center.
Donnie's her third boy.
No one knows where
the others are.

Linda's been parted from
her husband, Lou, for the
past fifteen years…he's the one
in the plaid shirt, all sunken
eyed, drooling, shaking.
They say it's delirium tremons.

On the end is Marcy's mom.
She's got her good blue dress on
and she doesn't need a hymnal:
she knows the liturgy by heart.

Donnie's Aunt Jean, the sweet
young thing in the ruffled dress
is godmother. Uncle Larry,
the pedophile in gray is godfather.

My Lord, Donnie's screaming louder
than a calliope and look how
he's writhing like a fish on
a hook right in front of the font!

Oh, thank God – there's the
benediction. Even the stained-
glass Jesus looks relieved.

Look at Marcy. All she's got to
show for family is the crumpled
bulletin in the bottom of her purse.

"We must embrace pain and burn it as fuel for our journey." -- Kenji Miyazawa

On Creativity

When I'm on fire
words dance over paper
hugging each line
in tandem with
my reflections.
Like fragile stems
or tips of petals,
they become a
solved puzzle
drawn thin in the
stiff embrace of
closed eyes. Silent
screams drown my
thoughts. Hurtful
words creep in
like mildew, gray
and brittle -- then
my pen glides over
the page. The sound
of rustling silk.

Flying With Sandra

I sat on the curb crying,
wished I was older,
wished I was safe
in the little red
house down the road.

Once I played among
the green hedges there.
Sandra was Wonder Woman.
I was Super Girl.
We used old silk scarves
as capes as we flew from
adventure to adventure.
We drew each one with
chalk on the sidewalks
and we never broke our
mother's backs! We
were too invincible.

He grabbed a fistful of hair,
dragged her into his yard.
Used her red paisley
scarf to silence her.
Pierced her, shook her,
with his body, eyes, laughter.

I stared at the countryside
absent from that place,
my cape draped softly
over my shoulders,
Then, I was flying with
Sandra to save the world.

Opal Tears

I brushed my hand
against your cheek,
caught each opal tear,
fiery on my fingertip.
Their salty essence
sponged into my skin.
I winced in pain,
wished my silent
gesture could free
it from your soul.

Easter 1957

On Easter, we visited my grandparents.
We left Good Friday in a gas-guzzling
green Plymouth, with big ugly tail fins
and eerie, leering chrome grille.
I saw Miss Kathleen and her kids
walking over to Ziggles old store.

Eight times a mother, Miss Kathleen,
thin, transparent, had an old diaper
wrapped around her head. Little Sandra
waved real hard. Miss Kathleen puffed
on her Chesterfield, smoke wisped
around the old diaper. She smiled.

Sandra, bright-eyed, grinning,
Shirley Temple curls,
still waved as I looked back.
Sandra always came on a rusty
red tricycle. We'd play dress-ups
down the basement in summer.
Winters, we played baby dolls,
springs, we flew cheap tissue
paper High Riders we'd get at Ziggles.

Easter Monday, we came back.

Early next day, as I skipped over
to Sandra's, I saw old chewing gum
stuck flat to the walk. Sandra's
brother, Raymond, used a pen knife
to scrape that stuff up last Tuesday.
Then he chewed it! Sandra and I, we
both screamed, Raymond laughed.

I looked up at Lowman's carbon copy
house, dark as a shroud, black
curtains drifted from jagged open windows.
Miss Kathleen's sofa lay upside down
out front, pink and green cellophane
grass clung among the dandelions.

They say Sandra and her sister, Diane,
were found hugging purple and yellow
Easter bunnies under their bed.
Raymond was found behind a garment
bag in a closet. Melted chocolate
eggs, charred straw baskets all over.

My fingers curled around the cold
chain link fence. I stared.

Now, a memory snapshot, I see
Sandra coming, tattered dress,
Fudge-sicle smile. I remember
when I hear squeaky wheels
coming down the walk.

Alice

I like that tree,
the one that needs
a haircut, she declared.
Pointed to the soft
green willow with
teared leaves
cascading into
the stream.

I'd like to read
a book there -
my back to its
trunk, a striped
cat watching from
a limb with a
Cheshire smile,
tail wound up like
a corn curl, with
white piano key teeth.

Then I'd yawn, flick
my golden hair
behind my ears
to hear the willow's
silent sobs.

Grief Has A Sound

Grief has a sound.
It comes in jagged streaks.
The mind is not an
obedient witness,
only poems and fragments
remain like fingers
gliding over a rosary.
Grief has a sound.
Long sleeping, it speaks
in layers; an alphabet
without vowels.

Vixen Hill

Before he went home,
Richard Cory may
have gone 'way over
to Vixen Hill, where
laughter floats like
curtains in the shade.
Exquisitely garbed
women pose still as
glass, hollow-eared,
wide-eyed. Their
carved men, polished
as patent leather,
search bone-tired
and bleary for warm
laps, pulsing with
sound; such scamps
they are, yet
the women, their
mouths drawn up like
artichokes, sip drink
after drink in the
seamless afternoon.
And Richard Cory?
Seeing no worth in it,
returned home and
slept with his revolver
that very night.

Vigil

(for Susan)

The Cancer book says
it's inflammatory,
five year survival
rate - forty percent.
You are so brave.
We fight the battle
together, yet I know
you feel alone.
I pray. You pray.
I touch your hand,
cry inside.
"You will not die,"
I declare, for I
need to convince
myself, too, as I
whistle in the dark.
I want to save
you, but only can
wait as an I.V.
drips into our
mortality. I
murmur, "sister, sister."

Walking At Holly Hill

Early snow clings
to dead leaves.
Squirrels dash
past headstones.
Falling backwards
in time, wordless
songs cover my
shoulders, a gray
wool shawl.
A reluctant shadow
is there, cloaked
in layers of space,
under a cloud-clotted
sky. Pieces of a
broken equation stake
a claim, spiral
through me, disappear.
A whisper in
a noisy room.

Painted Daisies

The painted daisies
have faded.
This morning, I
washed my long
hair, gathered
it into a towel.
I remembered
when you brushed
your hair one
last time.
Next spring,
the daisies will
bloom again.

Prophets

Mother of my father,
you knew the truth
all along: Prophets
were not popular,
so you did not speak.
In an old tin-type,
you folded your white
hands among the lilies,
rusty fall zinnias
smiled at your feet,
clovers beribboned
your thick, dark hair;
your eyes cradled in
a veil of dust, deep-set
and blue, you wore
your prayers as a shield.

Later, in one early December,
I looked upon Dad's face,
his cold hands buried
among the roses, the
stars and stripes draped
limply at his feet.
Unpopular, he raised his
voice and left me his legacy.

Some day, my scarred hands
will clasp carnations, delicate
and pink. My long red hair
will rest upon my shoulders.
Though silent, my voice will
be heard as my children look
to me to celebrate the painful,
delightful truths of their
own inheritance.

If Only...

If only I could
hold your hand
just once,
I'd smile
and with my
fingertip, I'd
trace each
line slowly.
God in His
wisdom made
only one of
you. I can
not trace the
same lines twice.

Words

Somewhere in small, dark, quiet places,
mysterious as Spanish moss, I spin
words into blurred but powerful patterns.
Words that are fierce and suggestive; words
flexible as wire, yet rigid as a priest.

When they come, gleaming bright as
pearls, living off moonflowers, they nest
in a world as vast as a coral reef.

My words hold translucent opal butterfly
secrets; sharp, thorny, opaque secrets;
deceitful, truthful, transparent secrets.

My words tell of a world of gentle pleasures,
of a land of seedy characters,
of a feral life of a woman on the run.

No one will ever know me, for I leave
nothing but words hollow as a coconut
or earth-friendly as a gardener who
turns over new sod in spring.

Night Watchman

Down Bolton Yard where
freight trains lined
up like dominos,
Joe inspected cantaloupes
and cabbages in
the dead of night.

From the corner of
his eye he saw
that thug, Enzo,
tramping in from
the other side of
the tracks; big handed,
filthy-faced, with
piercing eyes
glinting from beneath
his coarse woolen cap.

"Take a walk, Joe,"
he rasped. So
off Joe went, 'cause
he didn't want to
wind up on a meat
hook in a refrigerated
car bound for California.

Twenty minutes later,
Enzo caught up with
him near the receiving
office. "Got a light?"
he asked. Joe offered
him a sweat-stained
matchbook.

Enzo lit up, tossed
the matches back,
strolled from sight,
melting into the
shadows of the boxcars.

At dawn, on a
smoke break, Joe
found the fifty dollar bill.
It nearly fell from his
clammy hand as he
crammed it in his pocket.

He looked about him.
He knew the rules of
the Yard.
He'd get a present for
Stella, go home,
eat a late breakfast.

Louisville Slugger

"Ain't no one gonna rob
my house," he used to say.
Kept a Louisville Slugger
behind the bedroom door
next to the bed for assurance.

A trip to the john
in the wee hours brought
forth the moment of truth:
he spied the glowering
eyes peering into the window.

Bounding down the hall,
he snatched up his
weapon - came out swinging.
Then when the hand mirror
crashed into the tub,
the Slugger realized the
sinister face was his own.

Red Carpet Treatment

One year the railroad
gave Joe a big bonus.
After years of splintery
planks and cracked
linoleum, he declared,
"Now we got carpeting
like them rich people!"

Stella reveled in crimson
delight. Gleefully,
she buried her
toes into its thick,
generous, pile.

As the neighbors filed
through, they whispered
behind their hands
as they peered into
Stella's front room.

Even that gossipy old bird
Priscilla Lou Wentworth,
who got plastic on her
sofa last year, was at
a loss for words.

Mole Lady

Miss 'Lizbeth used
two fingers to part
her blinds so
she could peer
out at us.
Dad called her
the Mole Lady.

We imagined her
after a day of
nosing up mounds
of dirt, exposing
it to the light
of day, with a
pointy mud-caked snout.

Dad used to stand
in the yard to
wait, poised with
a spade till he saw
an underground disturbance.
Then he'd come down
hard and decapitate
his pesky prey.
Said it was easier
to get rid of the
garden variety than to
shut her up!

She thought no one
knew, but the soft
tunnel tracks leading
to her house
gave her away.

Kentucky Derby Clock

Stella never let him forget
how he lied to her.
Joe'd stopped at Mickey's
for a beer - was late.
Said he'd gone to see
the Derby on T.V.
A year passed by when
Joe sat on the couch
with Stella to watch
their newly acquired television.
The Kentucky Derby!!

"This is the first year
the Derby has ever
been televised," bragged
the race track official
from Churchill Downs.
"T.V. history!" sneered
Stella. "You lied to me!"
she ranted through her
obvious pristine perfection.

Forty years later, Joe gone,
a clock hangs above the
kitchen sink. "A peace
offering," Stella crows.
"It's my Kentucky Derby Clock."

Ivory Tower

That night Leroy
had a couple;
missed the trolley.
Back on Locust Lane,
Jewell saved a
dried-up dinner.
All day she'd crawled
along the baseboards
scrubbing away
with Ivory soap.
Leroy stomped up
the pavement, kicked
in the screen door
with his filthy
thick-soled boots.
"You lazy bitch!
All you do is sit
around all day,
gossiping, spending
all my money!"
In the steamy heat,
sweat dripping from
her eyelashes, hair
stuck to her head,
Jewell, she grabbed
a piece of Ironstone,
chucked it, dove
under the table.

They were the first
ones on the block
to get Melamine dishes.
Tonight Jewell's out there,
perched on the glider
studying the anthills
among the crabgrass.
The scent of Ivory soap
drifts from open windows.

Slick Raymond

Slick Raymond, a no account,
lived over North Point Village.
Foul-mouthed, greasy-haired,
dodged the cops, skirting the law.
Drove six different cars,
had but one set of tags for 'em all.

Hogged the whole alley,
so Rita got ticked off
and called the cops.
Slick spied 'em, took
the tags off his Chevy truck,
stuck 'em back on his
rusty green Caddy, so
it was all legal.

Snickering, he wiped his
nose on his sleeve,
gave Rita the finger,
then sauntered back
to the stoop of his rented
row house, lit up,
took a long drag,
Then turned on his C. B.

Dundalk Sabbath

Soapbox Sundays after church,
breakfast smells of eggs,
sausage, and coffee.
Weekly Father litanies over donuts.
Sunpaper in fist, pounding on table.
"Pigshit!" he exclaimed.
"They're a batch of bleeding heart
liberals! I say go in and get 'em!
Those damn commies will
never get this country!
Some lawyer thought of that!
Those rich sons of bitches in
the Valley lay on their lazy
asses while the working man down here...
We put cardboard in our shoes!
It was the Depression!
You're all spoiled! We never wasted!
We used Sears catalogues, by God, we did!
Camping out? I ain't doin' that!
I had enough camping out in World War II,
while I was in the Philippines!
Its a dog eat dog world! Don't trust
any of those bastards!"

Then tired silence settled like
the mesmerizing drifting smoke
that crept from his cigar.
Clad in his undershirt,
he stepped down from the podium.

The Dundalk Cowboys

Out in front of the green tiled
Arundel Ice Cream Shop in
Old Dundalk, they gathered
each morning, predictable as dew.
Their voices were of wars and
strikes, tobacco and coffee.
Poppies red as blood and
streamers of judgement dripped
over the pavement where beauty
was pulled out of thin air even
on pencil gray days in industrial
drizzle. Their clothes shook
about them like musty newspapers
as their conversations were
discarded by passers by like the
runny useless scrawl of trite
poems crumpled and stomped
for good measure into the
gutters of Shipping Place.

Our Heroes

Mr. Ron came over one day,
had his copy of the Eagle,
waved it right in Walt's face
over the chain link fence.

At dinner Walt complained,
"Payton's a big blowhard -
makes me sick listening to him
go on and on about that
no good son of his."

"This time, there's Jimmy
grinning smack in the middle
of the "Our Heroes" column,
decked out in his dress uniform
with Ole Glory flapping in the breeze
right behind him," he said.

"Seems Private Payton,
the little whiner from Little League
who used to slash tires and steal bicycles,
up and joined the army!
I can't believe that little snot
made it through boot camp!"

"Yeah, there was Ron, all puffed up,
boasting how Jimmy'd soon be
close by up at the Proving Ground
training to be a heavy duty mechanic."

Walt, smiled and
took it at the time, but later he spat,
"It's a shame the Viet Nam War
is almost over."

Six months later, Walt got all choked up
at breakfast when he read that
Jimmy Payton, War Hero, would return
home to his dad in a box.

"It was the armpit of the world." -- William W. Hellier, Sr.

Luzon, 1944

Before the war, Dad
loved to go hunting.
Never came home
empty-handed, so
he was a natural
for the infantry.
He came upon fields
full of rotten,
maggot-faced men,
friend and foe, alike;
carried a wounded
officer on his back
for two days in the heat,
stopped to relieve
himself. He said
he heard a snap,
looked up, saw the
enemy hiding
in a tree.
Their eyes met
momentarily, but
all Dad remembered
was this guy's face
flying everywhere.

He got a promotion
and a Purple Heart.
Came home -- never
went hunting again.

Paper Boat

Lottie, her name was Lottie,
said she was a Gold Star Mother.
She came to scrutinize the bake table
in white crocheted sweater,
peering at each item through thick,
blue plastic spectacles,
the kind with the rhinestones
embedded in the frames.
Black handbag dangled from her elbow,
her hair perched on her head
in neat, tight curls.
Says she eats at Woolworth each day,
doctor says she has to get out.
Since her son got killed in the war,
the days are lonely.
They treat her good at Woolworth,
even when she couldn't chew, they
fixed her food special, Praise the Lord!
"I miss him so," she sighed.
With a longing, empty look,
she bought a brownie.
Then Lottie meandered away,
like a fragile paper boat sailing
aimlessly on a big river
through the busy, churning mall,
filled with folks hurrying
to do their errands,
to rush home to the
constant demands of family life.

Obits and Pieces

Miss Nellie used to read the obits each week.
Only thing worth looking at, so she claimed.

On Thursday, the phone'd ring, and she'd
bend Grandma's ear, yapping about
all the deaths in Dundalk.

"Old man Florentino who owned
that big lumber yard - the one where
people can get fine oak and
expensive cherry... he just keeled over
and they hauled him off to City Hospital.
Says he must'a had a heart attack.

And Gertie Cavey - she's laid out at Bradley's.
You know - the old woman who sold snowballs
to neighbor kids from her basement on
Sollers Point Road...car hit her on Liberty Parkway
and there's a picture of the whole thing
right when it happened.

Remember Maggie Wokowski from Saint Luke's
Sodality? She'd worked at the Country Club
for fifteen years and bowled on Dottie's Dolls
with me at Pinland. She died in her sleep.
They even mentioned her high bowling
average and what a good gardener she was.

I graduated with Sylvester Reynolds and
the viewing's at Duda-Rucks.
He'd just retired from the National Brewery.
Liked to watch race cars and took his latest live-in
to Italy last spring!"

Grandma said she couldn't keep up with
all Nellie reported - she didn't know
any of those people.

Nellie's life was death.
When she died, no one even bothered to
put anything about her in the paper.

Down the Avenue

The Blue bus doors slapped open,
stomping aboard from the Avenue,
we threw our fare in the coinbox,
laughed as we slipped into
the torn leather back seat.
"Hey man, look at the mentals!"
some nasty creep shouted from a side seat.
We pointed our fingers at him,
howling insanely, laughing till
tears ran saltily into the
corners of our mouths, and we choked.
Aggressor, now victim himself,
he shut up, retreating to the streets.
Graffiti smeared walls sneered at us,
paper wads and litter swam
about our feet in the humidity.
Hot, we pulled down the windows.
Above the zooming roar of exhaust
fumes, we obnoxiously screamed
at the soggy pedestrians below,
"Hey, Look! It's raining!"
So we rode the MTA
as Baltimore pelted upon the roof,
down Eastern Avenue and into Highlandtown,
where everyone calls you Babe or Hon.

Matinee

"I'm 12," she lied.
Paid her quarter.
But her friend was
too tall, had to
pay 75 cents
to see the movie.
On the neon sidewalk,
we watched the movement
of the Strand's red
and yellow lights.
The line long,
aroma of greasy
popcorn beckoned.
It was amazing how
those soda machines
worked - push a
button, just enough
soda to fill a
flimsy plastic cup.
Wasn't worth ten cents.
Popcorn wasn't worth 15.
We raced up in the
balcony to see the
real show. Couples
made out in the back
row oblivious to us
brats up in front who
threw popcorn and soda
on the audience below,
then laughed, moved our
seats, avoiding the
usher's probing light.

Downstairs, we sucked
on hard sweet Jordan
almonds, mused over
posters of coming
attractions stapled
inside glass cubicles.

Later partitioned off,
mysterious balcony empty,
silent, the Strand,
a reminiscent relic,
voices echoing off
comedy and tragedy,
eerily peering from
ornate walls of velvet
curtains and gilded gold.
Its slanted floor leading
to a stage of dreams bought
for a quarter at Centre Place.

Sideshow

Curtis used to show
off for me that summer.
The top of a chain
link fence was
his tightrope,
balanced himself,
did tricks.
I never saw him.
After dinner in the
shadow of our ticky-
tacky house, I
watched the cars whiz
by for entertainment.
I sat on the slick
grey porch stoop as
rednecks cruised by
in cars with names
painted on them,
their elbows nonchalantly
hanging out windows
and cigarettes dangling
from the corners of
their mouths. Their
girlfriends snuggled
close in the middle
of the front seat.
I watched them all
and never paid attention.
I wondered where they
were rushing to as they
barreled by.
Curtis continued his show.
I never knew, for the
traffic never stopped.

Clover Chains

Down at the school ground
where beer bottles popped
up overnight like toadstools,
and graffiti washed away
in the acid rain, we wove
clovers into the tarry asphalt
breeze. Yard upon yard of
moppet catkins knotted by
tough waxy stems snaked
through the dandelions
butter soft and gold.
Crabgrass snapped at our
hems that clung to our legs
like steamy hot laundry
fresh from a wringer.
Days pushed by days
tumbling like cartwheels
down a stairless case.
In the shadow of the steel
mill, we tenaciously worked
obstinate little blooms into
unending fragrant chains.

North Point A La Carte

In the late 60's,
we junior high kids
used to hang out in
North Point's cafeteria.
We were obnoxious
and loud and our
enemies were serious
types whose faces
surely have turned
to stone by now.
The food was gross.
Lucky Debbie always
brown-bagged it.
We'd try to trade
our fare for one of
her Scooter Pies.
Janie had neither lunch
nor money, so we all
used to pitch in,
buy her lunch or
feed her part of ours.
The cafeteria food stuck
to our ribs and to
everything else!
Forkfuls of last year's
instant mashed potatoes
hung in gobs from the
ceiling, along with butter
pats from three years back
which were greasily silhouetted
on blinking fluorescent lights.

For fun, we'd throw green
rubbery Jello cubes down
and wait for old man Pulaski,
the Vice Principal, to slip on them.
Or we'd toss small foil
packets of ketchup
on the tiles and wait for
stylish Miss Rubins to
trot along in her high
heels and tight skirt.
She'd stomp the foil
just right, mash it,
and red gunk would
squirt everywhere.
We'd laugh and laugh over
our devilish deeds
amid piles of beat-up books,
runny cardboard milk cartons,
and gravy laden aluminum trays.

Patapsco Portrait

Down southeast Baltimore
we went through the motions
of public education.
Hungry stereotypic kids
battling landslide minds-
already-made-up-opinion.

"You hoodlums!" screeched
Mrs. Mu-Zak. Claimed
her minister husband
could save us from a
life of Dundalk Damnation.

"To Hell with you!"
sneered the fat chemistry teacher.
"I get paid anyway!" he slobbered,
guzzling Pepsi in the
September cinder block heat.
Shared torn lab books,
notes scribbled with yellow nubs,
perched on three-legged chairs,
we snickered knowingly
at dusty, empty blackboards.

Outside, the disposal plant
relentlessly chugged, coughing
graceful acrid vapors
into the stifling air.

With our red-neck labels
we prayed to Jude, played
Varsity with deflated equipment
donning mismatched
left leg shin guards.

Anemic gum-chewing cheerleaders
watched as we kicked and
pounded our opponents,
pink detention slips
clenched in our fists.

Lessons

With your voice
soft as nocturnal
silk, you once
told me we
connected.
You gave me
a book;
I devoured it,
seeking a
kindred spirit.
Now, in moments
of chipped glass
and purple thistles,
I watch the
pyracantha creep
along the wood pile.
The lilt of a mysterious
moonlight sonata
with the half-life of
a murmur settles
among the bleeding
hearts like a
flute on the wind.

Fantasy

I dream of dancing
in a sculpture garden.
Stars swarm above me.
My spirit swift as
water, wearing lapis
lazuli blue, moonstones
hanging from my ears,
I skip over snowstars.

Crickets sing a symphony
in darkness, thick as jam.
I press your face in
my warm hands, brush
my lips to your cheek.

My feet skim the soft
earth. Following your
voice of lavender and
doves, I sway to the
compelling rhythm of
a marvelous incantation,
like a lover possessed
with desires as prolific
as fireflies trolling the lawn.

Balticon '96

That night at the
Omni Hotel, the
bar patrons,
hollow as terra
cotta men, pivoted
about, sloshing
drinks like cheap
souvenirs. A lady
with glittered eyes
smiled a greasy
red smile, motioned
to the bartender
with her Rite Aid
acrylics, her
sequined bodice
shook as she laughed.
I glanced at my
pocket watch,
looked up. All that
was left of her was
a smeary cocktail glass.
A witness that
would never speak.

*Une Tranche De Vie**

She tossed back her fluffy hair,
slender *Gauloise* lifted to her lips,
wisps of smooth white smoke drifted
above her head, a melting halo.
In broken French, she ordered
*"une autre bouteille de chablis blanc."***
Toast after toast, cigarette ashes
mixed with ooo-la-las in Paris
where starlight persists in
the cafe nights and street
vendors sell strange, dark
flying toys that loop
bat-like beneath the glittery
heights of *la Tour Eiffel*.
Alcohol, tobacco, humidity
blended into a blur while
entranced sentinels stared
from perches atop Notre Dame.
Then, so late and quiet, life
was a question mark to study
in that incredible City of Light.

*A Slice of Life
**Another bottle of white Chablis

Bilingual

You did not
know me, but
you threw me
a wink. Few
take time to
learn my
language for
I'm always on
auto-pilot.
Subjects merely
shift, as a
reflex. You
say I came
from leftfield.
Once we walked
barefoot there,
my denim skirt
swirled about
my ankles.
I picked violets
and put them into
a woven basket
with my songs.
Now, you say you
do not understand.
Something must
have been lost
in the translation.

Boudicca*

Nowadays, I hide in suburbia
far from bickering spouses,
run-down launderettes,
beer stained walks and
Steel Town's industrial haze.

My former life, so fast speed
was but a color that blind-sided
me, was prophetic, wild, war faring.
With uplifted fist and flowing
red tresses tumbling in a great
mass to my knees, I picked trash
from the alleys, screamed orange
and yellow bestial oaths
unfit for children's ears.

In retreat, quasi-serene,
I feed the squirrels in my
hardwood castle, but Steel Town
cannot be forgotten. I can tell
you tales older than yew trees,
with morals that rival
the force of a catapult.

*Famed Celtic Queen who had the strength of ten men.

Winter Solstice

A plague of starlings
is on the lawn.
Weeks ago, the roses
folded their lips
and dropped their
scarlet coats.
Tumbling leaves
made their solemn
pact with an
early sunset as
it unfolded like
a fan in the west.
Frost air brushed
on a window pane
is but a forged
signature of
beauty to come.

After the Storm

A cold rain is ringing through my skull.
I'm clearing away old branches of hurt.
My legs, fluid smooth Slinkys,
my thoughts, sandy, gritty, edgy.
Words swirl about me, slip from my grasp
into a frigid pock-marked sky.
After things happen,
under the scarring, I'll heal.
They could make a movie about my life.
About the angel that walks along
the back of my hand,
bold as a run in a nylon.

About *Dundalk Proud*

"One can hear the sound of the Good Humor truck making its way through this book. Wendy Stevens looks back at the old neighborhood. Memories are recorded here like photographs taken by an aunt or uncle. Stevens gives us the sweet taste of summer and ripe watermelons. Here are poems that capture the way we were. Stevens remembers when she was Super Girl and the world was filled with working people who knew how to carry life on their shoulders."

  -- *E. Ethelbert Miller*
    Director of the African American Resource Center at Howard University, core faculty member of the Bennington Writing Seminars at Bennington College in Vermont, and author of several books including "Fathering Words: The Making of an African American Writer" and "Beyond the Frontier."

"To steal words from a poem in this wise collection, *Dundalk Proud* is beauty pulled out of thin air. Life hums and seethes in the shadows of the steel mills, and Stevens introduces the reader to her world with love and respect, as well as humor and some-times a heartbreaking clarity. Slip into these Dundalk poems and see how they touch you in places you thought you'd forgotten. Rough and tumble, indomitable poems, like a good Dundalk woman."

  -- *Barbara Westwood Diehl*
    Founding Editor, The Baltimore Review

More About *Dundalk Proud*

"The best poems are those that trade on the senses and sentiment, creating a vivid and emotional world. The poems in W.H. Stevens' first collection *Dundalk Proud* take us back to a world where young girls vied to be the "Mystery Beauty" while fathers came home exhausted from a day at the Point. Mothers stayed home and cooked and cleaned and the Saturday air was "laced with steamed/ crabs and beer." Not only does Stevens recreate the beauty and indomitable will of working class Dundalk after World War II, she also provides us with the living example of a writer who continues to grow and feel, a survivor who sits with her cancer-stricken sister and murmurs, "sister, sister." Stevens is a sister poet to all of us, a writer whose world is to be read and enjoyed."

  -- *Barbara M. Simon*
    President, Maryland State Poetry & Literary Society

"The poetry of W.H. Stevens is the poetry of life – her life, my life, everyone's life. Some of the verses made me cry, while others had me laughing out loud – in a room by myself! Ms. Stevens has the gift to make her words come alive, echoing the rhythms of street talk or the lyricism of nature. Allowing me to read these poems was Ms. Stevens' gift to me and us all."

  -- *Tracy Miller*
    English & American Studies Departments,
    Adjunct Faculty, Towson University